Usborne
Wipe-Clean
First Words

Use the wipe-clean pen to trace the
dotted lines to help the monsters
write their first words.

Illustrated by Kimberley Scott
Designed by Claire Ever. Words by Jessica Greenwell.

Monster town

Dressing up

hat   top

on   off   zip

Playing outside

bee

log

lit

cut

bug

ant

Monster kitchen

Monster sports day

On the beach

sun

rod

net

fin

A day at the farm

hen

pig

yap

dog

box

wet

in

tub

Finish the words

Help the monsters finish the words to match the pictures.
You can look back through the book if you get stuck.

h _____

c _____

n _____

b _____

a b c d e f g h i j k l m

h _____

b _____

p _____

f _____

v _____

Writing words

Help the monsters write the words to match the pictures.
You can look back through the book if you get stuck.

_____

_____

_____

_____